Presentation C[...]

Mount Saint Mary's College

With all good wishes

Theod[...] [signature]

April 30. 1968

WASHINGTON BOWED

Washington Bowed

BY

THEODORE R. McKELDIN

Governor of Maryland

MARYLAND HISTORICAL SOCIETY
BALTIMORE, MARYLAND
1956

DEDICATION

To Ted and Clara, my son and my daughter,
whose enthusiastic and continuing interest in the history of our land
is to me the pleasing promise that the future will seek wise guidance
and sound inspiration in our Nation's glorious past.

FOREWORD

Essentially history is experience. The combined experience of people covers an infinite range of activities, and there is little limit to the varieties of methods by which history is recorded. Frequently important historical facts can be gathered from an incident mentioned casually. If a story writer of a long time ago referred to a fork we know that even if his romantic tale is largely fiction, he knew the fork had come into use as a table utensil.

Biographies of outstanding men and women are indispensable in efforts to ascertain historical facts. There is, of course, the danger that in a biography, results of the work and influence of the person written about may be exaggerated, often unintentionally, and a true statement of relative values not given us.

Often a skillfully-narrated event in the life-time of a man will throw a flood of light upon his character, his achievements and the history generally of his times.

In *Washington Bowed*, Governor McKeldin has captured from the life of our first and greatest President a moment of ever-enduring significance to this Republic and to all nations —an historic incident which depicts in clear relief George Washington's faith in the ability of Americans to govern themselves.

Much of the value of this well-told tale, with its message emphasizing our justified trust in civil authority, lies in the fact the story has been little known—lost, perhaps, despite its own inspiring drama, in the understandable urge of many worthy writers of history to tell and retell the magnificent achievements of George Washington on the fields of battle, or when as first President of the United States, he was shaping wisely the general scope of that office.

Governor McKeldin is an instinctive and constructive historian. His research in history is for the love of the subject, and he adapts his findings to our times whenever he deems them pertinent. No doubt he handled this present work with some special affection because of his daily nearness to the narrative's scene.

Washington Bowed is delightful reading. It is an important contribution to the story of America — always wonderful — and as applicable today and tomorrow as it was when a distinguished group of men convened in Annapolis on that December day in 1783.

GEORGE L. RADCLIFFE
President, Maryland Historical Society

Acknowledgments

Washington Bowed first appeared in print in *American Heritage*.

The author takes this means of expressing his gratitude to the publishers of that excellent publication, and also to:

Miss Mary-Carter Roberts of the Maryland Department of Information.

Mr. James W. Foster, Director of the Maryland Historical Society.

Professor Elliott Coleman of The Johns Hopkins University.

Albert W. Quinn, Assistant to the Governor of Maryland.

Their valued assistance, including research and criticism, made this work possible and attests to the authenticity of the details.

I T WAS MY PRIVILEGE SOME TIME AGO
to discuss the fundamentals of American
government with President Eisenhower.
The course of the talk led inevitably to
George Washington. President Eisenhower
said that, in his view, the greatest hour of
Washington's life came at Valley Forge. The
President felt indeed that Washington's
achievement there had the quality of a
miracle and that Washington must be
thought of as a leader sent by God to the
young American nation struggling in its self-
creative, life-or-death war.

11 ·

I doubt that anyone will care to gainsay this. If Mr. Eisenhower, one of history's great generals, sees the miraculous in Washington's military accomplishments, it is not for the less experienced to disagree. On the contrary, a civilian may with profit turn his eyes on Washington's civil career, to see if he may discern similar evidences of Divine inspirations there.

It has been my own study to do this for some years, and I have satisfied myself on the subject. Acting to influence our nation's future, Washington so divested himself of the ambitions common to men in his position as to take on the semblance of an instrument of Providence. It seems to me today that we must think of him in that semblance, if, in the present world crisis, we are to believe, as most

Old Senate Chamber,
State House, Annapolis, Maryland
where Washington resigned his commission.

Washington resigning his commission as
Commander-in-Chief of the Continental Army
before the Continental Congress on December 23, 1783.

Painting in Maryland State House by Edwin White.

of us do, that the United States, under God, is the hope of humanity for a better life for more people everywhere.

Even as Washington personified greatness in his soldierly life, so he demonstrated it again and again in his civilian career.

I find his greatest moment indeed in a dramatic occasion of which I am reminded daily, as I go in and out of my office in the Maryland State House, for the Maryland State House was the scene. It was the occasion of Washington's resignation of his military commission.

It came just a year after the close of the Revolution. The date was December 23, 1783. Washington at that time was surrounded by popularity that was close to worship. Only a few men in history have been so rapturously

13 ·

taken to a nation's heart. Had he declared himself dictator, the American people by all indications would have been happy to have him. His response was to withdraw from public life entirely, acting not from a mere wish to enjoy a private existence once again, but from conviction that the national interest indicated his withdrawal. That this was his purpose he made clear, even to the present day, by the procedure he used. He not only resigned. He dramatized his resignation ever so slightly. It was never necessary for him to do much in that way. He was in himself so dramatic as to be virtually Drama. All contemporary accounts agree that he possessed magnificence, that his greatness spoke from his mere presence. He was vested in it. Consequently he was able to give drama to his

· 14

resignation, though the actual ceremony was neither long nor elaborate. It lasted less than an hour and was witnessed by not more than a hundred people—yet he made of it a decisively symbolic act in a time of national crisis.

For crisis there was. The war was won but the peace was not. Everything needed to be done and there was no one to do anything—this despite the fact that the nation possessed an incomparable galaxy of brilliant men. The trouble was in the organization.

The central authority was the Continental Congress, which, by its nature, was incapable of performing the necessary acts of national administration. To the incapacity, moreover, it was just then adding an epic indifference. Some states neglected to send any delegation, while few sent a complete one. Meeting after

15 ·

meeting disbanded for lack of a quorum. The opening date of the winter session of 1783 had been fixed for November 26th, and it was not until December 13th that enough members assembled to transact business. Even then only nine of the states were represented and two of these—New Hampshire and South Carolina —had to be discounted, as each had sent but one man. So it was actually a count of seven —Massachusetts, Rhode Island, Delaware, Pennsylvania, Maryland, Virginia, North Carolina—out of thirteen that could be called present and they only by reason of partial delegations. All together, they mustered just fifteen men.

Thomas Jefferson was one of these. So was James Monroe. So was Elbridge Gerry, so was James McHenry. Great minds, certainly. But

· 16

there was little that they could accomplish. The Continental Congress, in short, was without prestige. The people had virtually forgotten that a national body existed. Actually, the preceding summer, this national body had been obliged to flee from Philadelphia by reason of riots staged by disorderly soldiers demanding their unpaid wages. It had gone to Princeton, where it had finished the session. Then it had decided on Annapolis as its next place of assembly. There were two reasons for the decision. One was that Annapolis, by extending the courtesy of an invitation, seemed to promise a welcome. The other was that Maryland had a place where meetings could be safely held— a new, "commodious" State House.

Beside this distraction in the national legis-

17 ·

lature, the prestige of George Washington makes a wonderful contrast. Effectiveness was his aura. The war was won, the Army sent home, the enemy gone from our shores. To the people, it was as if he had done these things personally. Great as he has been in history, he was greater in life—he was looked up to as if he had been superman. His position, indeed, was one that has brought fatality to many free governments. He was the beloved Strong Man. He chose this time to visit Congress.

In Annapolis, it had taken for its meetings the Chamber of the Maryland State Senate. While it was holding its unhappy sessions there, Washington was advancing toward it in what was a veritable triumphal progress. He had let it be known that he intended to

return to private life. On December 4th, in
New York City, he had bidden his military
family a personal and professional farewell.
It was his expressed intention to take his
official farewell—to resign his commission—
when he reached Congress. But he had not yet
resigned it. He was still the general in fact
and he was the hero of the hour in the popular
estimation.

He had constant evidence of the latter con-
dition as he went along. In the three cities
through which he passed—Philadelphia,
Wilmington and Baltimore—he was joyously
received with townwide celebrations. To the
official welcomes, moreover, there was added
a frenzy of popular acclaim. How many men,
seeing a nation thus at their feet, have put
principle above ambition? *How many men who*

19 ·

knew themselves competent to rule—we may ask particularly. For there could have been assembled a good deal of plausible justification for a seizure of the power by a competent man just then. Washington could have told himself that the nation not only wanted him, but needed him. It has happened again and again in history that a liberator has fallen into such temptation—and ended as a tyrant. It could have happened to us, had God not vouchsafed us Washington. We cannot know his thoughts, as he rode, with his modest escort of two aides, through the wintry landscape. The record is, however, that he conducted himself not as the master of the country that was idolizing him, but as its servant.

The triumphal quality of his journey came to a climax as, on December 19th, he ap-

State House, Annapolis, Maryland,
the cornerstone of which was laid in 1772 by Sir Robert Eden,
last Colonial Governor of Maryland.

President Dwight D. Eisenhower,
in his office in the White House,
receiving the Maryland State flag from
Governor Theodore R. McKeldin.

proached Annapolis. He was met at a point
outside the city by a welcoming committee
of distinguished civil and military officers.
These gentlemen escorted him to the tavern
—Mann's, on Main Street—where lodgings
had been reserved for him. Thirteen cannon
were discharged in salute as he arrived. He
was in a position to hold a veritable court—
but he took no advantage of the fact. Instead,
early the next day, he made it his first official
act to go to pay *his* respects to the president
of the Congress.

A personal shading enters into this call,
that throws Washington's impregnable correctness into wonderful relief. For it happened that the president was Thomas Mifflin,
formerly a general of Washington's staff. He
had not rated highly in Washington's mili-

tary estimation. Washington, indeed, had felt that he had reason to suspect Mifflin's loyalty to himself. But Mifflin was now the chief civil officer of the government that Washington served and Washington unhesitatingly paid him deference.

The same day, December 20th, he sent a letter to Congress, asking permission to resign, and still with his awe-inspiring correctness, requesting that he be notified as to the manner in which Congress wished the resignation to be tendered—by writing or by audience. Congress in the meantime had been making its preparations. It had appointed Thomas Jefferson, Elbridge Gerry and James McHenry a committee to arrange the resignation ceremony.

These gentlemen established the protocol.

They advised Washington that he would be accorded a public audience and set the time for noon on the 23rd. He was to come accompanied by his aides, they informed him. On entering the Senate Chamber, he would be shown to a seat, they continued, but the aides should remain standing. The president of the Congress would tell him when he might speak. At the close of his address, he should return his commission to the president and hear the president's reply. Thus far went the stipulations for the routine of the ceremony. Added to them was a provision for the spirit. It said that, until the resignation was completed, the members of the Congress would remain seated and would keep their hats on. They were not to rise or to uncover to General Washington. When, however, General Washington had become Mr. Washington, then the Congressmen were to rise and lift their hats. But even then, the rule reads curiously, *they were not to bow*. They were to maintain their superiority to Washington, whether he were soldier or citizen.

Today, even keeping in mind the punctilio of the eighteenth century, anyone reading this record will feel that Congress' emphasis on its own dignity had a defensive quality. The hard fact had been that, before the members could act at all, they had had to decide by special vote that seven states were competent to deal with the subject, since the number required by law was actually nine.

But to George Washington seven states were sufficient. One state would have been, had that one in some manner been vested with

· 24

the law of the nation. Between the time he received Congress' instructions and that set for his audience lay three days, and those days were crowded with tributes to him. The Governor of Maryland and the Council of State sent him welcoming letters. The mayor and the municipality of Annapolis did the same. He received visits from all the distinguished people of the countryside. One act of his stands out significantly from this excitement of acclaim. It came at a public banquet in his honor, held on the 22nd.

In accordance with the fashion of the day, thirteen toasts were offered, each to the discharge of cannon. The last was "Long Health and Happiness to our Illustrious General." The illustrious general capped this. He offered, "Competent Powers to Congress for

25 ·

General Purposes," thus putting Congress' future above his own.

That same evening, the Maryland General Assembly gave a great ball in his honor in the "brilliantly illuminated" State House. Then, as well as the cheers of the men, he received the compliments of the ladies. He courteously danced every set. And the next day he presented himself at this same building—to resign.

As the audience was public, there were as many visitors as the Senate Chamber's limited space would accommodate. These, and the members, make a wonderful assemblage of great historic names. There were three of Maryland's four Signers—Charles Carroll, Thomas Stone, William Paca. There were two future Presidents — Thomas Jefferson and

James Monroe. There were four Revolutionary generals—Horatio Gates, Arthur St. Clair, William Smallwood and Thomas Mifflin. There were two future Cabinet members—James McHenry and Elbridge Gerry. There was the Governor of Maryland, likewise a Signer—William Paca. Officers of lesser rank though not of lesser glory made up the number. And before the eyes of all these servants of our country, George Washington, the first man of the land, played to perfection the servant's part.

He arrived at noon, as Congress had specified. He came accompanied by his two aides. He took the seat assigned him. He waited for the president's permission to speak. Then he read his address. It was brief, as his public utterances always were, but it conveyed his

27 ·

customary firmness. No one could doubt its sincerity. His resignation was real, not a gesture. At its end, he "drew out from his bosom" his commission and placed the document in the president's hands. Thus, at every point, he conformed to the rules of the Congress, whose members were keeping their hats on in his presence. And so the ceremony was ended, and Washington was General Washington no more.

Then Congress did finally rise and uncover as a sign of respect to him. And then Washington performed his first act as a private citizen. It, too, was a recognition of Congress' authority. He returned Congress' mark of respect with a greater one. He bowed, as Congress had specified he should. That was the consummate dramatic touch. We can imagine his grave and measured stateliness.

An illustrious historian of my state has called this bow of his a "self-abnegation." I disagree. To me it was nothing faintly negative. It was Washington's affirmation of government by the elected representatives of the people. He had fought a war to secure this benefit for his country. He would not do other than support his creation.

I believe, furthermore, that all the spectators understood his meaning—for how else can we explain the emotion that followed? Every account says the onlookers wept. They were Anglo-Saxons, they were men used to danger and schooled to self-control. But Washington's noble dignity carried the ceremony to that height where self-forgetfulness is the needed response. And these contem-

29 ·

poraries of his were not ashamed to follow.

Today the room where this portentous drama occurred is kept by the State of Maryland as a virtual shrine. The place where Washington stood is marked. The rest is as it was then. There is the platform with the president's desk. There are the desks and chairs of the members. There are the visitors' spaces, where so many great and brilliant people of the day assembled. Only one addition has been made. That is a magnificent portrait of Washington in his hour of victory —at Yorktown—done by a great artist— Charles Willson Peale.

It is my privilege as Maryland's Governor to work near this chamber, and I sometimes stop beside the grill that guards the door through which Washington entered, and look

· 30

in. It is not necessary to imagine the scene.
In that still and beautiful room, the presences
seem always to be. And, as I see them in my
mind's eye, the moment is inevitably the
same—the one in which George Washington
bowed. I shall always think that was his
greatest hour.

PRESS OF
SCHNEIDEREITH & SONS
BALTIMORE, MD.